Time to Practice:
A Companion for Parents

A guided parenting journal
designed to foster discoveries
about you and your child
through your musical journey together

By Carrie Reuning-Hummel

Grateful acknowledgement is made to the following for permission to reprint previously published materials.

Adaptation from *Live the Life You Love* by Barbara Sher, copyright © 1996 by Barbara Sher. Used by permission of Dell Publishing, a division of Random House, Inc.

Charts from within pp. 38-51 from *Raising Your Spirited Child Workbook* by Mary Sheedy Kurcinka, copyright © 1998 by Mary Sheedy Kurcinka. Reprinted by permission of HarperCollins Publishers.

Charts from within pp. 20-22 and pg. 35 from *Point of Power* by Kay Snow-Davis, copyright © 2005 by Kay Snow-Davis. Reprinted by permission of Sage Publishers.

Published in the United States by Sound Carries Press, Ithaca, New York.
www.soundcarries.com

Editing by Pamela Moss

Cover artwork by Kristen Slater

Graphic design by Torri Bennington

Photo of the author by Jan Regan

Library of Congress Control Number: 2006906692

ISBN – 13: 9780978673406
ISBN – 10: 0-9786734-0-9

To my daughter Sarah:

I cannot thank you enough for
being on this journey with me

Contents

Acknowledgements ii
Intellectual Debts iii
Introduction....................v
Suzuki....................viii
My Experiences with Dr. Suzuki ix

SECTION ONE: DISCOVERY

Being Seen....................2
Parent Discipline 3
Creating Space 5
Motivation 6
Temperaments 8
Energetic Rhythms 12
Gifts 18
Learning Styles....................22
6 Philosophies to Look At Before Moving On: 24
- 1-The Quest to Learn
- 2-A Look at Rewards
- 3-Turning Weaknesses Into Strengths
- 4-Underlying Assumptions
- 5-Expectations vs. Vision
- 6-Asset vs. Deficit Thinking

Decision Making....................33
Here is What I Know About Myself and My Child....................34

SECTION TWO: THE PRACTICE

Creating the Conditions 38
Practice Organization....................40
Taking Temperaments Into Consideration in Our Practice....................45
Using Motivation, Energetic Rhythms, and Gifts in Our Practice 47
Practicing Principles....................50
Fostering Ownership of the Instrument from Day One 55
Taking a Step Back As Our Child Progresses....................57
When You Know the Practice is Going To Be Rough 59
Action Plan/Goals/Thoughts....................60
Practice Planner....................64

Bibliography....................68
About the Author 70
Order Form....................71

Acknowledgements

Deepest gratitude to those who have made my work and this book possible:

Therese and Jen for listening and guiding, gently and respectfully

My Suzuki friends for supporting me and laughing with me all of these years – especially Teri and David Einfeldt

Jae and Kelle for putting me back together after my car accident, and then sending me off on a new path while they were at it

My parents, Sandy and Joan Reuning, for providing a rich environment to grow up in

My husband, Eric, and my children, Sarah and Benjamin – words cannot express what you all mean to me

Intellectual Debts

Dr. Shinichi Suzuki

Mary Sheedy Kurcinka, who wrote *Raising Your Spirited Child*, and saved me from feeling like I was a bad mother

Barbara Sher, who wrote *Live The Life You Love*, and framed how I think about motivations and gifts

Alfie Kohn, who wrote *Punished By Rewards* and *Unconditional Parenting*, and turned my thinking around about rewards and even praise

Dawna Markova, who wrote *The Smart Parenting Revolution* – a book that I wish I had as a new parent

Kay Snow-Davis, author of *Point Of Power*, who has taught me so much about myself and my family, and become a friend as well

Introduction

WHENEVER I READ OR HEAR someone's thoughts on a subject of interest to me, I find it helpful to have some insight into their perspective. For this reason I want to share some background information about myself.

I am the oldest of four children, born to high school sweethearts and wonderful violinists. Until I was five, life was pretty ordinary. My parents were public school string teachers who had recently begun teaching at Ithaca College. They were hard workers who put family at the top of their priorities.

Then, in 1964, the first tour group of violin-playing Suzuki students came to the United States from Japan. They were lead by Shinichi Suzuki himself, a great man who saw the wonderful potential in children. My parents attended one of the concerts in Philadelphia and were moved to tears by the excellence and heart exhibited by these young children. They knew they had to learn more.

After the five hour car ride home where they decided to make this method their life's work, they asked me if I would like to play the violin. I was enthusiastic about it, so they started a tiny class of beginners ranging in age from three to five years old. I was the oldest at five and a half.

Everything took time. The violins needed to be ordered from Japan since there were no small ones available in the United States. My parents quickly found that it was very different to begin a five-year-old child (or a four or three year old!) on an instrument than the more typical eleven or twelve-year-old beginner. They obtained the music books from Japan, but of course all of Suzuki's helpful advice was in Japanese!

Fortunately, Suzuki traveled to this country many times to help all the interested teachers get started. Any time he came to our area I would have a lesson with him on a stage with many teachers looking on. I am embarrassed now with how I looked! I was very skinny with not the best physique for the violin, so my violin posture was quite droopy. I had a "pixie" haircut with crooked bangs, blue pointy glasses with sequins, and skinny legs usually covered with calamine lotion because I was so allergic to poison ivy. Somehow, Suzuki looked beyond all that. I always felt nurtured in his presence.

From that time on, not much about my childhood was ordinary. My family, imbued with a pioneering spirit, traveled all around – my parents gave talks about Suzuki's philosophy while my siblings and I played for these audiences. One time stands out in my memory, when my two little sisters played the

Bach Double Concerto, 1st movement, at a university. I believe they must have been eight and six years old at the time. The college students' (and professors') mouths were hanging open with astonishment.

At fifteen years old I had the opportunity to go to Japan with my parents. I had many lessons with Dr. Suzuki, spent social time with him and his wife Waltraud, and played in concerts with Japanese children. It was an amazing experience to know the same pieces as these children with whom I could not speak. It really opened my eyes to the universal language of music, especially when the shared Suzuki repertoire was part of the experience.

When I returned home I began teaching private students, and at nineteen years old began teaching at summer institutes and workshops. In my mid-twenties I began training other teachers. I suppose I could have been considered quite a Suzuki "expert" at that point, but once I became a parent I realized that I knew nothing at all!

I think that I came into parenting as prepared as one could be. I had worked with countless parent/child Suzuki partnerships, taught in a Suzuki pre-school, received a psychology degree with an emphasis in child development, and read voraciously about educational philosophies and parenting. I waited until my early thirties to start my family, chose a fantastic parenting partner, and found ways to develop my career while being home with my children.

Even with this training ground, I still was not prepared for the intensity of my parenting journey. I don't think I am very different from most parents in having that deep-down, mind-numbing fear of being an inadequate parent. I also don't think that I am alone in my discovery of the deep reservoir of love I have for my children, and therefore with how seriously I am taking this journey.

When my children grew old enough to take on a musical instrument, I gave a lot of thought to the decision of early Suzuki training for them. I knew that I wanted them to be able to express themselves musically, and that there was no better way to do so than to start early and follow the Suzuki philosophy. I also knew that this would require a lot of me, and this felt daunting. What lead me to the final, unequivocal decision to start them on musical instruments (my daughter on cello and my son on violin) was that I wanted the same close learning partnership with my kids that I had and still have with my parents.

Now that my children are fourteen and sixteen years old, I feel I have gained small kernels of wisdom that have helped to bridge my lifelong preparation for parenthood with the reality of the day-to-day parenting experience (including practicing music with them). I have learned as much or more from the practicing challenges as the practicing successes.

I also draw upon the perspective that I have gained from 30 years of teaching. Over this time I have seen that children are changing. We often hear of the negatives that accompany these changes: that children need to be entertained, that they have shorter attention spans, or that they are less respectful. Certainly there is a grain of truth to all of this, but what I see is that there is much that is positive about the change. Children of today question things. They want to see *why* they are being asked to do something, and they want to see how one thing relates to another. Gone is the unquestioning adherence to authority. This might look messier, but it gives me great hope that these children will begin to move our world in a new direction.

With these ideas in mind, perhaps we need to approach practicing with our children a little differently than in the past. We need to discover who they are and let them take ownership of their learning and direct it for themselves. Music provides a perfect opportunity to do this.

My hope is that sharing this journey will help parents who are now in the trenches of practicing with their children. This workbook is organized into two parts. The first section addresses how we can make discoveries about ourselves and our children that I wish I had known about from day one as a parent. The second is organized so that a parent can take what they have learned in the first section and apply it to the actual practice sessions. The manual is designed for *any* parent who practices anything with their child, not just the Suzuki parent. I will make frequent references to Dr. Suzuki because of how helpful he has been to me and countless others.

We are so fortunate to be on this path with our children! It gives us a unique chance to look at our own gifts and those of our children, examine our motivations, and find out how we learn.

Have a lot of fun with these discoveries!

Suzuki

Dr. Shinichi Suzuki (1898 – 1998) began his method for teaching violin to very young children in Japan after World War II. His teaching model was to look at the way that all children learn their native languages and to help them learn music in the same way. The main premise is that we all are musical—we are all born with talent. If we begin quite young so that our ears can absorb the sounds, if our parents offer encouragement at home, and if the general environment is such that we can be steeped in the experience, there is no stopping any of us from exceeding all expectations and fully reaching our potential. Dr. Suzuki brought Japanese children playing the violin to the United States in 1964. Music education has not been the same since!

Suzuki education is offered for violin, viola, cello, bass, piano, flute, guitar, harp, recorder, organ, Suzuki in the Schools, and early childhood education.

For more information on the Suzuki Method™:

www.suzukiassociation.org

Ability Development From Age Zero by Shinichi Suzuki (Senzay Edition/Ability Development: 1981)

Nurtured by Love: The Classic Approach to Talent Education by Shinichi Suzuki (Summy Birchard: 1983)

My Experiences With Dr. Suzuki

I SEE DR. SUZUKI AS ONE OF THOSE SPECIAL human beings who was truly a great man. He was ahead of his time with his ideas, he was single-minded in his purpose, and he saw and brought out the best in people.

As a child, I *felt* him as much as I saw him. I felt his heart and his total respect for me as a person; he did not see me as just some kid standing before him having a violin lesson. I felt his energy shimmer in the air when I was near him. I felt his childlike delight in the moments unfolding in front of us.

I saw how the adults around me – the violin teachers – respected him. He expanded their ideas about music education (and education in general), indeed almost exploded them, to take in a new view of excellence.

And then there was the Suzuki I never knew because of my age and the language barrier, the man I have only glimpsed through others: he was a philosopher, a healer, a leader of the human potential movement, and a great thinker.

He saw the essential before most saw it. All children can speak their language fluently. Why not take this amazing innate capacity for learning something so complex almost effortlessly and apply it to the development of other abilities? Why not bring out the best that he saw in people? Why not little children? Why not musical talent? Why not beautify a world which needs hope and help?

What happened was that the world *was* beautified by his work, and not only because music offered by little children uplifts us. These children *become excellence.* They see that they are capable, that they have gifts to offer to the world. And the world is being transformed daily by this solid knowledge.

Where does it lead? None of us know, but the more I know about the man, the more I think that he had the vision to see where we were heading. I often think that if each child were truly seen and known as I was through Dr. Suzuki's eyes, this would be a dramatically better world.

Discovery

Being Seen

As I mentioned in the introduction, I had the experience of working with Dr. Suzuki numerous times as a little girl. Although I could not have put it into words at the time, he made a profound impact on me. As I had my violin lessons with him, I felt a mutual connection and a deep respect unlike anything else I had ever experienced. I felt that he was truly seeing *me* in our time together. This early experience has motivated me to find a way for all children to be seen in this same way.

Another important time for me was when I was 15 years old. At this point in my life I was fortunate to find many adults who saw me as a valuable person with valuable things to say. These people were vital in allowing me to develop the self-confidence I needed to express myself.

Take a moment now and think back in your own life.
Who took the time to really and truly know who you were?
What kind of impact did this have on you?

The person who saw me ______________________

Traits this person had:

Do these traits match yours? Often we recognize traits in others that we have ourselves!

It is unusual for the parent to be the person who truly sees their own child. What a gift it would be if we could do this within our own families! TAKE A MOMENT to imagine what our world would be like if our children were seen as valuable, with valuable ideas. What if they all were respected for the unique gifts that they bring? What if you saw your children this way, distinct from your hopes and fears for them?

Parent Discipline

It is often said that we can only be the best parents for our kids if we put ourselves first (an analogy from airplane emergency instructions is that you must put on your own oxygen mask first before helping your child). I have heard this advice many times and understood it intellectually, but never really thought it possible for me. Then I realized that this concept was a discipline for me. It took discipline to meet my own needs, because my automatic way is to meet *only* the needs of others. Little by little – certainly with baby steps at first – I tried out the idea. I started by eating better when I realized that I have a tendency to snap at my kids when my blood sugar is low. Then I tried getting more sleep. Both of these actions had huge payoffs, motivating me to continue them even when it wasn't convenient to do so.

Write about what needs to happen so that you are at your best. More sleep? Exercise? Time for yourself? Different eating habits?

I have especially found that having time for myself is crucial for me and for those I live with. In particular I tend to need "leaf" time (see Energetic Rhythms) where I just putter around the house and let my mind float wherever it wants. If I go too long without allowing myself this time I start feeling off-kilter. I see this time for myself as getting out of my busy mind (where I am keeping track of many things at once, most logistical) and "tuning" my mind to a different frequency, a different "radio station." All kinds of insights have come to me from this place; but mostly it keeps me sane.

Here is a simple meditation written by my friend, Therese Conway Killen (Gananoque, ON 613-382-0008), a flower essence practitioner and personal development coach. I have found it helpful to easily get me into a less jangled frequency.

This is an exercise we can use daily in order to feel connected to our own compass. We are part of an integral web that we can tap into if we are present to it.

MEDITATION

First, bring your attention to your entire spine. Focus on your tailbone area. Feel yourself comfortably engaging with your environment just as you are.

Next, bring your focus to your solar plexus area. Feel your body tuning itself to the proper frequency for you (sort of like tuning your body as you would a radio). Allow yourself to be with that sense of focus for a few moments or minutes.

Now feel yourself being surrounded by a clear boundary, like a bubble. Feel yourself filling your boundaries with your own energy. This will allow you to move and think freely.

Now that you have set your physical/spiritual intent to reach out into the world as your authentic self, you can listen to your body and soul for guidance and direction.

For More Information:

The Essence of Parenting by Anne Johnson and Vic Goodman (The Crossroads Publishing Company: 1998)
The last I had heard, this book was out of print. I certainly think that needs to change! This is a beautiful and wise book where I found deep truths about disciplining and nurturing ourselves to be the people and the parents we would wish to be. A sample of a couple of the chapters: *It Is Very Hard To Be Responsive To Others When We Are Being Unresponsive To Ourselves* and *Much Of Our Frustration And Difficulty In Parenting Is A Function Of Our Own Unresolved Conflicts And Emotions, Not Our Children's Behavior.*

Creating Space

IN THIS PROCESS of developing the discipline to put yourself first, you find little ways of doing things for you and you alone. For instance, you might find time to read a book! (And I'm not necessarily talking about a parenting book!) Or maybe there's time for a bath, or a walk, or a solo museum visit or concert. . . . Suddenly, these are not impossibilities at all. It's amazing how creative you can get when this discipline is in place.

The next job is to help your children create some space for themselves. This will probably take some discipline on your part as well. We all have an easier time discovering our gifts if we have some unstructured time in which to dream and play. This might mean that we, as parents, need to put a limit on the structured activities that we all take part in. It might mean that we may become advocates for less homework and less testing in schools. It might even mean allowing our children a little boredom now and then. Our family has found that some of our most creative moments have come from that uncomfortable feeling of having "nothing to do" – something many of us in our society try to avoid at all costs. What if this feeling isn't so bad at all?

Some ways we can create space in our busy life:

Motivation

As I began to quiet my mind through discipline, I began to have many insights about myself and my children. One exercise that I found to be very valuable was rating the following external motivators (from Barbara Sher's *Live The Life You Love.* Dell Publishing: 1996, pages 27-28, adapted).

Try doing this for yourself. Circle the most appropriate response.

	HIGHLY MOTIVATING ("A")		("C")		LEAST MOTIVATING ("F")
Praise	*	*	*	*	*
Positive Thinking	*	*	*	*	*
Guilt	*	*	*	*	*
Spirituality	*	*	*	*	*
Competition	*	*	*	*	*
Taking Classes	*	*	*	*	*
Ridicule	*	*	*	*	*
Grades	*	*	*	*	*
Lecturing *(as in "you always leave the door open, how many times have I told you....")*	*	*	*	*	*
Others:	*	*	*	*	*
	*	*	*	*	*

I found two very important things out about myself through this exercise. The first was that I gave an "F" to lecturing. Being lectured to by anyone makes me want to run away! So why would I think that lecturing my children would have any good results? The second revelation was that I had to give a "C" to guilt. This was not because I liked it any better than lecturing – in fact I hated it – but because I was largely motivated by guilt. Guilt was dictating many of my choices and actions.

My next decision was not a baby step – it was a HUGE leap.

I decided to give up making my decisions based on guilt as my motivator. This decision did not magically take away the things that still had to be done but weren't fun to do; however, much changed for me in this process. For example, it is time for bed and the kitchen is still a mess. This is really one of my biggest "drudgery jobs." The old me – run by guilt – would have slugged away at it, hating every minute of it, run by this guilty idea (who knows where I got it) that the kitchen *had* to be cleaned up before bed. The new me, not running on guilt, asks myself, "Why would I want to do this now?" My answer is, "Because I like to wake up in the morning and have a clean kitchen." It may sound rather silly, but it is an entirely different experience to clean the kitchen with an intention of giving myself the gift of a clean kitchen in the morning than to clean it resentfully out of guilt. The drudgery index goes way down.

Write down any discoveries you have made about you and your child's motivators.
Are they the same? Different?

What might you change based on your discoveries?

What can you see that is working already with the motivators in your day-to-day life?

Temperaments

My first child Sarah was one of those really easy babies – slept through the night very early on, had a great sense of humor, and was easily entertained. I have to admit that I did a certain amount of patting myself on the back during her babyhood. I felt that I knew what I was doing, since I had so much preparation with my Suzuki background.

Around the time Sarah was 18 months old and was starting to speak, my sweet little girl started arguing with much that I had to say. I didn't know what to make of it. I began little by little to wonder if it had something to do with my parenting.

A low point that is etched in my memory came when Sarah was about three and a half years old. She had a play-date at a preschool friend's house. When it came time for me to pick her up I did all the "right" things as a parent. I pleasantly told her that she had 5 minutes to finish up the puzzle she was working on, and then gave her another little reminder just before it was time to leave. Well, it did not go well. I ended up dragging her out kicking and screaming. As I looked back to thank the mother (who I did not know well) I saw a flicker of an expression that said to me, "You don't know what you are doing." The dreaded "you are a bad mother" look!

I got very depressed after that because I thought she must be right. Why was it that when my sister asked her two children to get their coats on they would just trot right over, get their coats on, and happily leave? I knew I was raising my child in the same way that she was. Why wasn't it working?

Fortunately it was not very long after that event that I discovered Mary Sheedy Kurcinka's wonderful book, *Raising Your Spirited Child* (HarperCollins: 1991). What I discovered there was that while Sarah did not fit the definition of a "spirited child", she rated high scores in two of the areas typical of "spirited" children: she is very intense and not comfortable with adapting. No wonder! This explained everything! For instance, at her friend's house she felt intensely that she had never, ever had such a *wonderful* time, and she couldn't believe that her mother was taking her away from it! And her discomfort with adapting made her sure that she would never, ever have such a good time again.

These discoveries made a real difference for us. First, I felt such a sense of relief that my daughter's behavior was not a reflection of me being a bad parent. Secondly, I was able to become a coach to help Sarah with skills that she could use for the rest of her life.

So, the next time Sarah was going to a friend's house it looked something like this:

On the way to the house I tell her that it might be difficult for her when she sees me arrive to pick her up, but I promise to arrive as late as I can so that she has every possible minute to play. Then, to help her ease the transition, I let her know that we can go visit Daddy at his school on the way home. (This was one of her favorite things to do and helped her to feel that there are other fun places to visit besides her friend's house.) I do not use it as a reward (i.e. "If you are good about leaving then we can go see Daddy") but as a transition tool. Finally, right before going to pick her up I would give a quick phone call to the parent, saying that I was on my way and asking the parent to get Sarah's coat on, etc.

Through all of this I was amazed to discover that *I* was intense and slow to adapt as well, and started to see how we played off of each other. This led to more and more discoveries about the dynamics of our family, and more of a feeling that we are all exactly as we are uniquely *meant* to be. (Thank you, Mary Sheedy Kurcinka!)

Use the chart below to assess where your family members fall in the temperament continuum.

INTENSITY – *How deeply and powerfully are emotions experienced? Is every emotional reaction mild or intense?*

	Mild				Intense
Your Child	*	*	*	*	*
Yourself	*	*	*	*	*

PERSISTENCE – *If you tell your child to stop doing something that interests him or he wants to finish, does he stop or fight to continue? Now ask the same question of yourself.*

	Easily Stops				Pushes to Continue
Your Child	*	*	*	*	*
Yourself	*	*	*	*	*

SENSITIVITY – *Think about your child's reaction to slight noises, emotions, changes in temperature, tastes, and textures. Does he react to certain foods, tags in clothing, irritating noises, or other people's stress?*

	Low				High
Your Child	*	*	*	*	*
Yourself	*	*	*	*	*

PERCEPTIVENESS – *How easily do outside stimuli interfere with or change the direction of your child's behavior? How aware is she of people, colors, noises, and objects around her? Does she frequently forget to do what is asked because something else catches her attention? How about you?*

	Low				High
Your Child	*	*	*	*	*
Yourself	*	*	*	*	*

ADAPTABILITY – *How quickly does your child adapt to changes in his schedule or routine? How does he cope with surprises? How easy is it for him to shift from one activity to another? How about you?*

	Adapts Quickly				Slow To Adapt
Your Child	*	*	*	*	*
Yourself	*	*	*	*	*

REGULARITY – *Is your child quite regular about eating, sleeping, and other bodily functions? How about you?*

	Regular				Irregular
Your Child	*	*	*	*	*
Yourself	*	*	*	*	*

ENERGY – *Is your child always on the move and busy or quiet and quiescent? Does he need to run, jump, and use his whole body in order to feel good?*

	Low				High
Your Child	*	*	*	*	*
Yourself	*	*	*	*	*

FIRST REACTION – *What is your child's first reaction when she is asked to meet new people, try a new activity or idea, or go someplace new? What's yours?*

	Jumps Right In				Rejects At First
Your Child	*	*	*	*	*
Yourself	*	*	*	*	*

DISPOSITION – *Is your child more sunny or serious? What about you?*

	Sunny				Serious
Your Child	*	*	*	*	*
Yourself	*	*	*	*	*

The top three trigger traits (traits which are the most difficult to handle) for myself and my child:

MYSELF

1.

2.

3.

MY CHILD

1.

2.

3.

It is also helpful when looking at temperaments to discover whether we are extroverts or introverts. The best way to look at these two types is to determine where we draw our energy from. Extroverts, who make up the majority of the population of our society, draw upon others for their energy. They like to interact with people and talk things out. When they are depleted, they seek out social interaction. Introverts get their energy from within themselves. They refuel by being by themselves or with one other person. They can easily become overwhelmed in large social gatherings.

Notes on family members:

Extroverted:	*Signs of this:*
Introverted:	*Signs of this:*

FOR MORE INFORMATION:

Raising Your Spirited Child by Mary Sheedy Kurcinka (HarperCollins: 1991)

Raising Your Spirited Child Workbook by Mary Sheedy Kurcinka (HarperCollins: 1998)

The Hidden Gifts Of The Introverted Child by Marti Olsen Laney (Workman Publishing Company: 2005)
We live in a society where extroverts outnumber introverts by three to one and where we tend to value the traits of the extrovert. I learned so much from this book: that there is a continuum from introverted to extroverted; that most people stay with the temperament traits that they demonstrate at about four months old; and that there are biological differences between extroverts and introverts – differences in the actual brain function. Even though the title signals a close look at introversion, I actually learned a lot about both types through Laney's comparisons.

Energetic Rhythms

Just as we are all born with our own, unique fingerprints, DNA, and temperaments, we also have our own way of moving through our life – our own "energetic rhythm."

Learning about temperaments when Sarah was quite small made a huge difference for us. But when she was twelve years old I again felt that there was more for me to learn. We seemed to be constantly butting heads. I was at a loss to try and understand how we could be so different. I would bring up my confusion to friends who would give a knowing smile and say, "Ah, the teenage years! Just hang on and it will all be over in a few years!" I knew that it did not have to be like that. I simply had something to learn.

Fortunately, one friend told me that she thought that Kay Snow-Davis in Hawaii could help me. I arranged a telephone conference call with Kay and found the information I had been looking for. When I hung up the phone (at almost midnight because of the time difference) I understood exactly *how* Sarah and I were different. And when I told Sarah about it the next morning she was so relieved. I remember her saying something like, "Now I see I don't have to be like you."

A number of years ago, Kay identified unique energies in different people. Defining energies is fascinating because energy is invisible (like music which is also a form of energy) and therefore difficult to talk about. At first Kay lacked a vocabulary for explaining what she felt intuitively. Finally, she came upon the analogy of the parts of a tree. I love this symbol because it is an easy way to talk about this nebulous area. The metaphor of the tree – which we all recognize – makes the idea of different types of energy accessible to us all.

We all are made up of four types of energy, symbolized by the four parts of a tree – the Root, the Trunk, the Branch, and the Leaf. These energies are the ways in which we move through the world. Each of us has what Kay refers to as a "Point of Power" – a place where the energies are in their most natural and unique state, which create our own personal "song". Our unique energy pattern consists of different combinations of the Leaf, Branch, Trunk, and Root.

In my family we each exhibit our own unique rhythm. Our creativity expresses itself differently for each of us. I find that describing each of us helps me explain the different types of energies. You may have more than one type of energy, more than one part of the tree that creates your natural rhythm.

Sarah's natural rhythm is the energy of the Root. The Root is the be-er, the do-er, in the moment; the athlete who loves the feeling of the running, the farmer who feels the earth as he or she works – these are Root energies in action. What was very difficult for me to grasp, having a different energy than Sarah, was that Sarah was playing the cello simply to play the cello. She was not trying to get ready for her lesson, learn the next piece, or prepare for the recital. It did not work when I imposed my own suggestion of a motivation, such as, "Let's learn this and surprise your teacher." The "Root" is not about words or philosophizing. It is about feeling this moment in time; it is the energy of form – that which is concrete, that we can see and touch.

My husband, Eric, manifests the energy of the Trunk, which also functions through the energy of tangible form. Trunk energy is goal-oriented, directed towards completing tasks to accomplish goals. The completion of a goal is what makes a Trunk's heart sing. They do not like lots of options given at the eleventh hour. Roadblocks can be very frustrating for them. They are happiest implementing and completing. Trunk energy is what gets the job done.

Branch energy begins to take us out of the solidity of form. It is actually about the formless being translated into form. I am a Branch, and what allows my heart to sing are *ideas*. But I want the ideas to have a relationship to life on the earth, so I am excited to translate these ideas, to connect them, and to bring them to form. However, it is not so much the bringing to form that I love (like the trunk), it is the *ideas*. Branches tend to have many more ideas than actual accomplishments, which can sometimes frustrate them or look like laziness to others.

Leaf energy is about the formless – perceptions and sensations. My son, Benjamin, has quite a lot of Leaf energy. The person who has their Point of Power in Leaf may have three "movies", scenarios, or potentialities playing simultaneously in their head. They might be in a conversation and take what someone said and spin off on it in their mind, only to return in a different place later in the conversation. Kay feels that many more children are now being born as Leaves – maybe because our earth is in desperate need of a new perspective. The adult Leaf performs well in a "think tank" situation where they come up with innovative ideas that can be implemented by another department. The "Leafy" child might have no interest in completing worksheets or following others' directions; Leaf energy often clashes with the structure of school, which is the structure of Trunk energy. We have a great responsibility to respect and learn from these children, as well as to figure out how society can adapt to them instead of labeling them and trying to change them.

So what I have learned with Sarah is that since she and I live in a different part of the tree with our energy it takes more communication to understand each other. I have learned that when I pick her up from horseback riding, she isn't being rude when she doesn't have anything to say about the experience, because it was so rooted in form that it has not had time to bubble up to her consciousness yet. She will tell me about it in an hour or two. Sarah is learning that just because I have all kinds of options to suggest to her it doesn't mean that I think her choice is wrong. We have learned that "meeting in the middle" (for us, in Trunk energy) often makes a huge difference.

Kay suggests that it is healthiest to be in our unique Point of Power 80 percent of the day when possible. This can be rather scary when our Point of Power is not Trunk energy, which is the kind of energy that best fits our societal norms because it is directed towards completing tasks. For example, with my Branch energy I find that if I allow myself to let go of the idea that I must "get things done" to be productive, and if I allow myself instead to be in my natural rhythm, then paradoxically I accomplish more with less stress.

Energetic Rhythms

the "tree" model

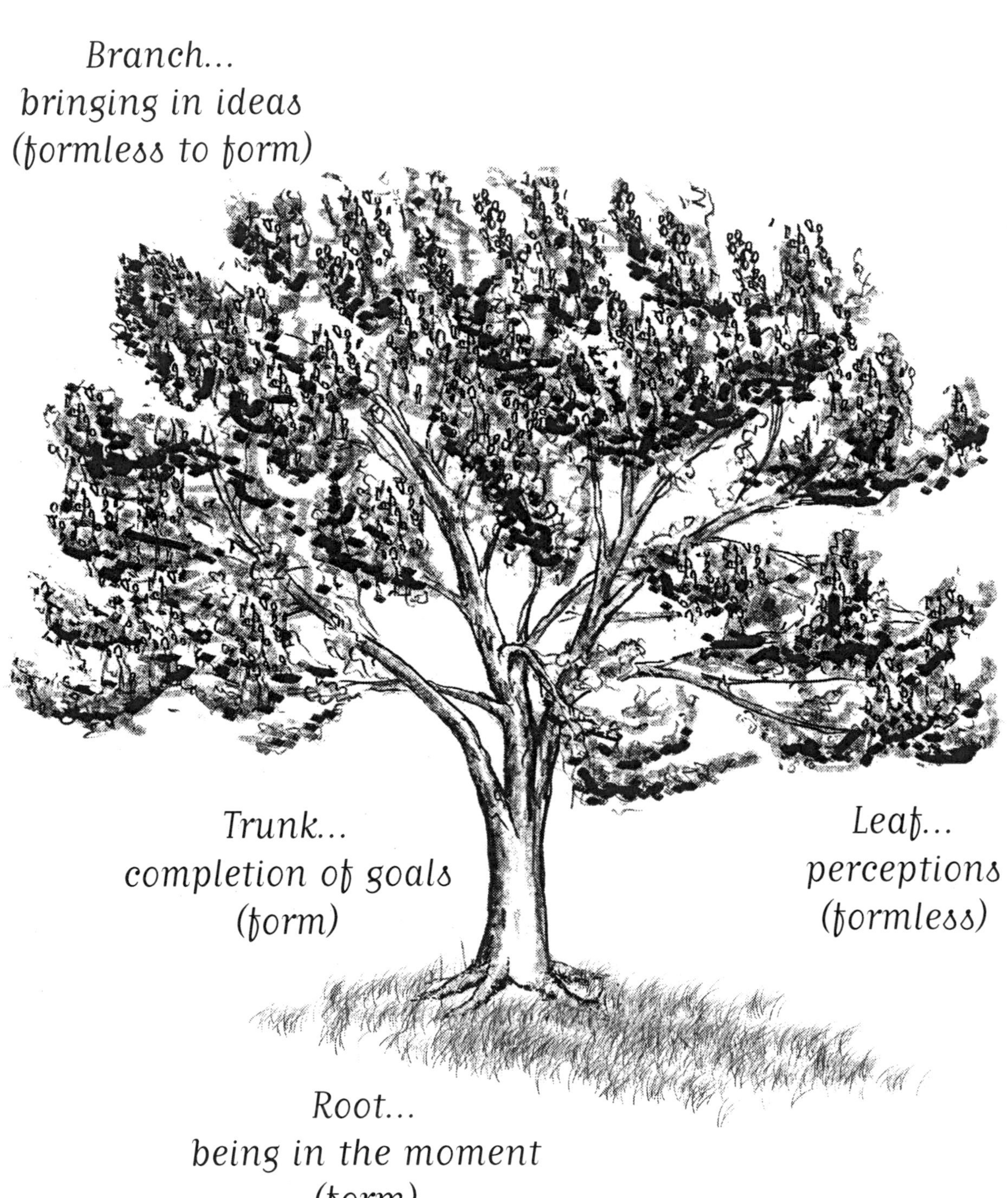

Here is a very simplified questionnaire and chart to help you discover where your family's energetic rhythms lie. Kay has written an entire book on the subject, which of course allows her to go much more into depth with the complexities of the subject – *Point Of Power: A Relationship With Your Soul* by Kay Snow-Davis (Sage Publishers: 2005).

LEAVES

- I have lots of ideas that never get completed.
- I have difficulty staying focused during conversations.
- It is easy and fun for me to do more than one thing at a time.
- I have concerns about making commitments for fear I'll miss out on something else, or I'll have to be responsible for that commitment.
- I'm fearful of sharing my ideas with others because they think I am unrealistic.
- Many times I leave a trail of unfinished projects as I move through the day (laundry, painting, lawn care, etc).

BRANCHES

- After I create something, I begin to lose interest in it.
- I'm always open and looking for my next "new project."
- I like to have freedom to create in my own way and at my own pace.
- When I am involved in a project I am open to new input and ideas, as long as I am not required to follow other ideas to the exclusion of my own.
- I can be interrupted and still maintain and return to my focus.
- Some people consider me inconsistent in my work world.

TRUNK

- I resent being interrupted in my projects.
- I like to do things "my way."
- I need to experience change in my life at a slow, steady pace to feel safe.
- I like consistency in my life.
- It is fun for me to put the details of life together in an orderly way.
- I like having a schedule in my life.

ROOTS

- I like to be by myself with the earth and nature.
- I like to observe and live life, not philosophize about it.
- People accuse me of being shy, stubborn and uncommunicative.
- I like to live simply.
- I like to go about my day undisturbed.
- There is a lot more to my sensitive nature than most people realize.

Point of Power Rhythms

DO ANY OF THESE REPRESENT YOUR POINT OF POWER?
If not, use the blank chart and draw your own representation.

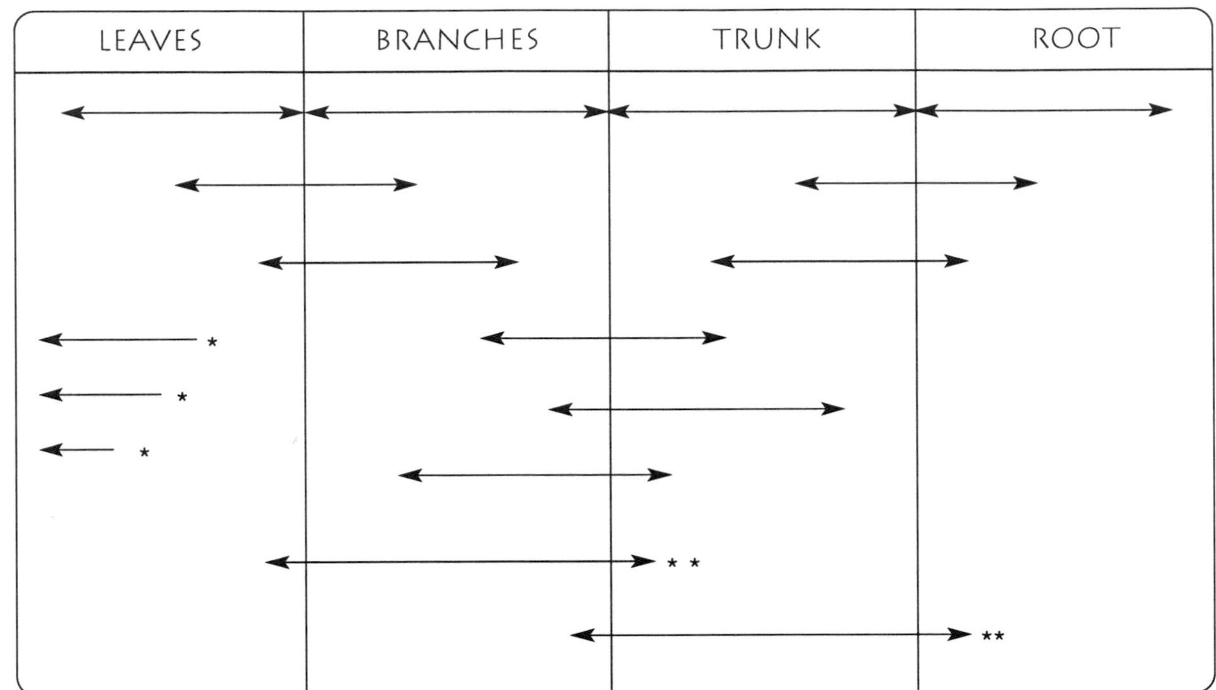

** These are Leaves who basically have a minimal relationship with implementation – they may appear confused, when in fact they are living in a more formless reality than many others. They truly have difficulty functioning in a mundane, daily life.*

*** A person may have a point of power that extends through three rhythms. These points of power combinations are created by rhythms that are adjacent.*

Chart Your Own Rhythm Below.

LEAVES	BRANCHES	TRUNK	ROOT

Chart Your Child's Rhythm Below.

LEAVES	BRANCHES	TRUNK	ROOT

Gifts

As adults in my life took the time to know me when I was young, I found that I was more apt to use my unique gifts. As we have seen, we all have motivations, temperaments, and energetic rhythms that make up our uniqueness. We also have our very own gifts that we bring to the world. I learned a lot about my own when I had a car accident 8 years ago. I was unable to play the violin or viola for almost 2 years due to a whiplash injury I received in the collision. Friends and colleagues would approach me and say in mournful tones, "How awful for you not to be able to play!" I would reply rather sheepishly, "Well, actually, I don't miss it much at all."

Around that time I discovered Barbara Sher's brilliant little book, *Live the Life You Love* (Dell Publishing: 1996). In it she refers to *skills* (or talents) as the things that you are good at (I was trained to be an excellent violinist, for example), but *gifts* as the things that you love and are driven to use to be fulfilled. Another way of saying this is that if someone took your gifts away from you, you would suffer. I quickly realized that if someone told me I could not be around children, or that I could not talk about the things that excite me, I would be devastated. These are a couple of the gifts that I am here to use.

As soon as I began to recognize my own gifts, I found it much easier to see my children's gifts. They have given me thousands of clues that I began to see as soon as I had an unclouded view of myself. Since then I have been learning to distinguish my children's skills or talents from their gifts. For example, my son is a very "talented" violinist, having received excellent training pretty much from birth. But one of his greatest gifts is in social interactions, in his love of people and his kind spirit. It has been important to recognize that it is this social aspect of his violin playing – sharing music with his friends or enjoying the sounds of a big group – that is important to him. The moment the focus is shifted to performing for performing's sake, he begins to be unhappy. It is a subtle shift, but an important one to be aware of.

Here are several exercises that will offer clues to your gifts, and the gifts of your child. Feel free to choose one exercise that suits you best or to use all three if you like.

MEMORY:

Close your eyes, go back in time, and see a memory of yourself in childhood, totally absorbed in the moment. Do you recall any colors, sounds, smells, tastes, textures, or other sensations of this moment? What were you focused on? What about it held your attention? How did you feel? Write about this memory. Then try this same exercise thinking of your child in your memory.

Myself:

My Child:

PHOTOGRAPH:

Go back through old photo albums and choose a photo that tells the real story of you or your child. Write about it.

3 BIG THINGS:

According to Mark Ylvisaker and Tim Feeney, brain-injury specialists who wrote *Collaborative Brain Injury Intervention: Positive Everyday Routines* (Singular: 1998), each of us has three big things that we care about. These are the things that matter most to us in our life as it is now. These three big things can really tell a story as well.

My three big things:

1 ______________________________

2 ______________________________

3 ______________________________

My child's three big things:

Ask your child what their three big things are. Maybe they will answer, "Playing with my dolls, my family, and running with my puppy."

1 ______________________________

2 ______________________________

3 ______________________________

NOW, "MINE FOR GOLD" WITH THESE EXERCISES:

What nuggets of truth have you found for yourself and your children? Some possible starting points are:

Were you or your child...

- outdoors/indoors?
- alone/with people/with animals?
- with one person/with a group of people?
- using hands?
- speaking/listening/using eyes?
- using imagination?
- performing?
- helping?
- moving/ physically active?

WHAT I HAVE LEARNED ABOUT MYSELF:

WHAT I HAVE LEARNED ABOUT MY CHILD:

For More Information:

Live The Life You Love by Barbara Sher (Dell Publishing: 1996)
This is not just another "how to" book! It might look like that from the cover, but this little book has a depth that I did not expect. Finding it when I was confronting some basic questions about what I am doing here on earth, I was propelled on a journey where I looked at my motivations, gifts, and what was blocking me from moving forward. Barbara Sher gives many practical steps for taking action based on the discoveries you make. I think that is what makes this book so powerful.

Learning Styles

I had planned on writing a detailed chapter about learning styles here, but have decided against it for two reasons. First, the subject is incredibly vast, and so many people have done important work in describing the complex inner workings of the brain. Much of this research has been incredibly helpful, but none can come even close to a full understanding of the human brain.

The other reason that I am not truly addressing this subject is because, in my view, the fact that we are talking about music here changes the "rules" of learning theories. Different people use different neurological pathways to achieve the same results, particularly in music.

Here is an example. A child plays *Go Tell Aunt Rhody* on the violin. What is she thinking as she is playing? Here are some possibilities that I thought of:

- Simply singing (in her mind) with a direct physical connection to the left fingers and bow
- Saying or singing note names (in her mind)
- Saying or singing finger numbers (in her mind)
- Saying or singing words to the song (in her mind)
- Imagining a color
- Thinking about a story or a mood
- Seeing the actual notes from the page (as in photographic memory)
- Feeling just how the fingers feel to be in the correct position
- Noticing how the "correct" (in tune) vibrations (versus the out-of-tune ones) feel in the body
- Repeating the teacher's or parent's instructions to herself, either to remember them or to resist them

These are examples I came up within a five minute span of time. I am sure there are more possibilities. Can you imagine how the brain would be "lit up" in different ways for these different examples?

I will never forget working with a student who had the "problem" of looking upwards as he played the violin. I had been trying to fix this habit for about three years when I finally thought to ask him what he was seeing. He answered, "Well of course I am seeing the notes go by as the scroll of paper they are on unrolls. And of course each note is its own color (the A's red etc.)." The most amazing thing about this for me was that he assumed everyone saw this as they played!

I would like to share some books below that have been a help to me in determining the learning styles of my own children, myself, and my students. What I want to encourage you to see is that we all have our own learning strengths. As we encourage our children to know these and use them, their so-called deficits can take a proper backseat.

For More Information:

7 Kinds of Smart: Identifying and Developing Your Many Intelligences by Thomas Armstrong (Plume: 1993)

Multiple Intelligences: The Theory In Practice by Howard Gardner (Basic Books: 1993)

Liberating Everyday Genius by Mary-Elaine Jacobsen (Ballantine:1999)

A Mind At A Time by Mel Levine (Simon & Schuster: 2002)

How Your Child ***Is*** *Smart* by Dawna Markova (Conari Press: 1992)

Discover Your Child's Learning Style by Mariaemma Willis and Victoria Kindle Hodson (Prima Lifestyles: 1999)

The Smart Parenting Revolution by Dawna Markova (Ballantine Books: 2005)
Of particular interest to me in this valuable book was a section on "Thinking Talents" (pages 151-167). Markova lists 36 talents that we can draw from, with five or so being our own. When I discovered my own "Thinking Talents" (love of learning, humor, excitement about ideas, connection, collaboration, focus, and optimism), I found that simply knowing about them enhanced my abilities. These talents are drawn from our abilities to be analytical, procedural, innovative, and relational.

Refuse to Choose by Barbara Sher (Rodale Books: 2006)
This is a wonderful book that Barbara Sher has written to describe people she calls "scanners". These are people who have interests in many areas or revolving areas and tend to move on to the next thing before completion of projects. I related to much of the book and love her positive approach to a trait that tends to be frowned upon in our society. A great book if you have a Leaf or a Branch in your family!

6 *Philosophies* TO LOOK AT BEFORE MOVING ON...

1

The Quest To Learn

It is worth taking the time to look at our basic beliefs about our children. We are passionate learners from birth. We all know how young children can be relentless in their quest to gain knowledge. I will never forget a spring day when my daughter and I were waiting for Daddy to play a concert that she was too wiggly to sit through. The reason that she was extra-wiggly that day, I think, was that she had just learned how to walk (not crawl!) up the stairs on her own two feet. When you think of it, that really is a momentous event in someone's life! So we went outside the chapel where the concert was being held, to a huge bank of stairs. Up, up, up, we slowly walked – Sarah holding onto my left hand. At the top we turned around, switched hands, and headed back down. I decided that since our ride home was with my husband who was still playing the concert, I would freely go with Sarah's wishes instead of imparting my own agenda. She kept on with this routine for an hour and a half, thrilled to be mastering her new skill, and reluctantly stopped only when the concert ended.

What has been exciting for me to find is that we are all essentially "wired" to be passionate learners throughout our lives. Sometimes outside factors can mask our passion for learning. Examples of this are letting concern about a test score override interest in learning a subject, or getting so exhausted doing things for others that we lose enthusiasm for our own path. But I believe that though our passion may seem buried at times, it is always there and ready to be accessed.

Possible roadblocks that interrupt our natural passionate learning:

- TV and computers (electronics)
- Grades and test scores
- People's views about us
- Concerns about looking good or fitting in
- Deciding that something is boring
- Lack of physical well-being (exhaustion, sickness, stress, being very out of shape)
- Feeling unsafe
- Over-scheduling — no time for play and self-discovery
- Too much structure, such as bells ringing to stop what we are doing

ROADBLOCKS:

What gets in the way of my passionate learning?

What gets in the way of my child's passionate learning?

FOR MORE INFORMATION:

The Passionate Learner by Robert L. Fried (Beacon Press: 2002)

The Inner Game of Tennis by W. Timothy Gallwey (Random House: 1997)

Any book by John Holt (see Bibliography)
Through careful observation of natural learning in children, John Holt became an advocate for removing the roadblocks that prevent passionate learning. All of his books are interesting reading for those who look at the nature of learning and education.

2
A Look At Rewards

If we are seen for who we are and allowed to use our gifts, we will be motivated, happy, and fulfilled. The child who is having a tantrum is not inherently manipulative or "bad," but is someone who is not being seen in that moment and has no other way to express this fact. As soon as we understand this, we find that we are looking at the child and not the problem. This shift in focus can make all the difference.

I had a flash of insight during a massage a number of years ago. I was totally lost in another world, when the massage therapist murmured, "Great energy." I was immediately taken out of my completely absorbed-in-the-moment state and began wondering, "I wonder if she says that to everyone. Does everybody have great energy, or am I unique? What was I doing when I had that great energy? Can I duplicate that now?"

After that experience I began to wonder if praising my students and my children was always the proper choice in the long run. Around the same time I came across the book *Punished By Rewards* by Alfie Kohn (Mariner Books:1999). He shows how research points out again and again that rewards are *not* the positive flip-side of negative punishment. In fact, they do not deliver in the way that our society "thinks" at all.

An often duplicated experiment goes this way: A child (or adult) is placed in a room with a puzzle and is told that in ten minutes the monitor will be back and if the puzzle is completed the child will receive "x" (a reward found to be meaningful such as money or candy). Another child is placed in another room with the same puzzle, told only to have fun with the puzzle and the monitor would be back in the same 10 minutes. What happens is that the child who is being rewarded is either in tears of frustration that he cannot finish in time, or he has finished and is sitting watching the clock. The other child is finished and is happily repeating the puzzle faster and faster, or trying new ideas out with it.

There is a joke that has been around for a number of years now:

> *What's the difference between a traditional teacher and a Suzuki teacher?*
>
> The traditional teacher says, "This is wrong, this is wrong, and this is wrong." The Suzuki teacher says, "Very good! This is wrong, this is wrong, and this is wrong."

It is a good discipline to check in with ourselves and see what the praise or compliment is really about. It is one thing when we are purely appreciating what our child has done, and quite another if we are saying it with the intention that we want them to do it again "for us." It is a subtle difference with a major consequence. We also must keep in mind that even with simple appreciation as our intent, the child might fall into the same mental trap as I did in my massage. Instead of being absorbed in the intrinsic pleasure of learning in the moment, the child is apt to be taken out of that moment and begin to think, "How can I please this person?" (if not something more negative).

So if we believe that our children are "wired" as human beings to be passionate learners, how can we support them?

> Playing a musical instrument is very difficult. How can we help, if we feel we are not "allowed" to compliment? I prefer to think of the whole practicing experience as something that I am not doing to them or expecting of them. I like to think of it as a partnership and an exploration of their learning process. If I see it like this I can offer feedback that is appropriate for the moment. This can work well, even if we are not musicians ourselves. Instead of, "You are practicing very nicely today," it might be "What did you feel like that time? That music touched my heart in a different way," or "That bow hold shape looked rounder to me." That way they are going to be more likely to want to hear from you, and you are much more helpful to them.

Another way to be with your child is to simply see and appreciate. Less is more with what we say to our kids. Sometimes just being companionably in the same room can be the best thing of all.

Now, this does not mean that you cannot show enthusiasm for the hard work *anyone* in your family is putting forth. But it is a very different thing to go out to dinner to celebrate a difficult hurdle successfully jumped, than to say, "If you finish this music book I will take you out to dinner", or "If you have a good lesson/practice/concert I will give you 'x'." It really is possible to go through parenting life without using rewards. I have done so, and I am very happy with the results.

For More Information:

Punished By Rewards by Alfie Kohn (Mariner Books: 1999)

Unconditional Parenting by Alfie Kohn (Atria Books: 2005)
This is a book that I wish I'd had as a new parent for help in defining my parenting philosophy. Alfie Kohn helps us to look at the bigger picture with our children: what do we truly want for them, and how can we get there? He continually challenges us to ask if our actions are consistent with our beliefs.

As in his well-known *Punished By Rewards*, Alfie backs up his statements here with extensive research. He honors the complicated journey of parenting that we embark upon when we operate from a place of utmost respect for our children. (It is much more difficult than, "Because I said so!") This book caused me to question and think more deeply about my beliefs and actions than any parenting book I have ever discovered.

3

Turning Weaknesses Into Strengths

We have been taught to avoid weakness at all costs in our society. Often we continue behavior that is not advantageous to us simply because we have refused to acknowledge the weakness that is driving the action. It is easy to see why we tend to operate this way. Since we know that revealing what we don't know leads to not getting the "A", we try to make it look like we *do* know. I was very much like this in my violin lessons as a kid. Instead of showing my teacher that I had a weak fourth finger on my left hand, I would vibrate like crazy when I got to it to hide my weakness. Why not go in and say, "I am not happy with the lack of strength in my little finger. Could you give me some exercises so that I can start building the strength?" I did not take on this role until much later – into my twenties.

What I find interesting here is how much we can learn from our weaknesses, and how they can in fact be turned into our strengths. For example, many drug and alcohol counselors were formerly drug and alcohol abusers. In my own case, some of my greatest strengths come from my greatest weaknesses. One example is my weak left hand. Although I did not become a hot-shot virtuoso violinist because of it, I learned how to teach left hand principles through the need to study them myself. Another example is from my early days of teaching. Since I began teaching when I was fifteen, I always felt a little weak working with the parents of my students. I felt like, "Who am I to tell them what to do when I am 10, 15, 20 years younger with no children of my own?" What I did was to dive into learning more and more about parenting, and work on speaking to parents with respect and a true honoring of what I saw them doing. My weakness in this area was transformed into a strength that has become an important part of who I am. I now feel that our weaknesses, just as much as our strengths, give us many clues about who we are capable of being.

Most of us are knowledgeable about defining our weaknesses, but we can get uncomfortable truly looking at them and seeing their ramifications in our life. Try out this chart and see where it takes you!

WEAKNESSES:	STRENGTHS:

4

Underlying Assumptions

Anytime you have an automatic thought about what you should or shouldn't do to be considered a good parent, that "should" is a warning that you are assuming something. It merits examination: is what you're assuming true, like a fact? Does it cause anxiety and stress and disempower you, or does it leave you feeling freer and more connected to your kids?

I examine beliefs about being a "good parent" as if I'm looking at rocks (sometimes as large as boulders!), picking them up, and seeing what's underneath. There are so many of these beliefs floating around our society – and we tend to take many at face value and never question them.

Let me give some examples, in no particular order:

- I must take something homemade to the school function. All the other mothers will be doing that. I will look __________ if I do not.
- Is my child going to be qualified to go to Harvard? Is her transcript/portfolio diverse/full/excellent enough? (I love how Alfie Kohn calls this "preparation 'H.'")
- If my child says something rude to me it means she is a rude person. That might mean I am a _________ parent.
- I must enroll my child in the same (or at least as many) activities as my neighbors' kids, otherwise I am ________.
- My child will go nowhere, achieve nothing, if I do not have expectations of her. (see next page)

The beliefs above may not "hit you where you live." Add your own assumptions about being a good parent below. Do you know where they come from?

ASSUMPTION:	WHERE IT COMES FROM:

Don't worry if you don't know where the underlying assumptions came from. I don't think many of us do. Some seem to just float out there.

For More Information:

Kids, Parents, and Power Struggles by Mary Sheedy Kurcinka (Harper Paperbacks: 2001)
This book helps us take a closer look at our fears as parents. Mary helps us to see the true *cause* of power struggles so that we can become "emotion coaches" for our children as well as ourselves.

5

Expectations vs. Vision

Dr. Suzuki was once asked how he could be so patient with his students. His answer was that patience is merely a lack of expectation. I love that. So many people have complimented me on my patience over the years. The word always puzzled me. I have never, ever felt like a patient person. I somehow equate that with putting up with something that it takes patience to put up with. This is not what I do. When I teach I feel like I am exploring. If a student is not able to master something right away I am interested in exploring other avenues to open up that door. To me that has nothing to do with patience. If they are just "sloughing off" and being lazy or difficult I am not particularly patient either. I try to find out if there is something else going on that contributes to this (like a difficult home life), and if not, I tell them to get busy and work!

A lack of expectation works very well, actually. It does not imply a lack of *vision*. No one I have ever met held a long-term, beautiful vision as Dr. Suzuki did. A small example of vision is to see a student who today is playing "Twinkle, Twinkle Little Star" someday playing a concerto with ease and beauty. We can hold this vision in every lesson or every practice while exploring in the moment.

It has been very helpful for me to have visions for myself, my family as a whole, and my children. It's a wonderful conversation to have with all the members of your family so that all can be supportive of one another.

VISIONS I HOLD:

EXPECTATION TO BE FREE OF:

VISIONS THAT MY CHILD HOLDS FOR THE FUTURE:

6
Asset vs. Deficit Thinking

In a society, which is often deficit-oriented, it can be empowering to live in an asset-based way. Our babies and toddlers live that way. When she falls down, or he reaches for the air instead of the cup that he planned to grab, neither tallies these as mistakes. Each sees the event simply as a step along the way to figuring out how to walk or to pick up the cup.

We can do this for our children when we are at the parent/teacher conference and we guide the conversation to what our child is good at.

We can do this for ourselves when we see that when we have had a practice with our child that didn't work, there is something we can learn for next time.

I love the idea that the further we move towards what works, the less monumental the problem becomes.

My friend Jae Atchley, a chiropractor and forward-thinking alternative health practitioner, wrote me this e-mail about a new way of thinking about health (or anything else, really):

> *"If we think in terms of moving with what works vs. trying to figure out the problem, we are always assured movement. If we move far enough, the "problem" becomes smaller and smaller without ever even doing anything to it. If we move far enough it may not even be perceptible. So we have expanded our perception, created more options, and eliminated that which was an obstacle for us. This means that there is always a solution to anything. If we move far enough we begin to experience that solution."*
>
> (For more information on Jae's work, see *www.universalhealthmethod.com*)

This brings to mind an "ah-ha" moment I had several years ago after hearing a parent talk by Carole Bigler, a renowned Suzuki teacher and piano pedagogue.

In order to illustrate the idea of "what you look for is what you see," Carole set the scene of early morning before school. Mark comes down the stairs on time, all dressed, his organized backpack in tow, with a sunny smile on his face. His mom immediately points out that he needs to tuck in his shirt. A little of the sun goes out of his smile.

What I realized after hearing this was that, particularly with my daughter, I tended to see the flaws that I needed to "fix" instead of the beauty in her. After hearing Carole's talk, I began to simply see Sarah as the truly sweet person she is instead of noticing the little negatives. It was amazing. By simply *seeing* (not saying a thing) it was like a light was shined on her sweetness. The little negatives took a backseat; they became shadows of themselves. I have found that this shift in my own perspective makes a huge difference for everyone in my family as well as with my students. What an easy "fix"!

For More Information:

The Smart Parenting Revolution by Dawna Markova (Ballantine Books: 2005)
Once in a while I come across a book I wish had been around when my children were young. This is one of them. Dawna Markova sees that each one of us is born with our own unique potential and that each of us is driven to reach this. What I love about this book is that she ushers us from formless philosophy to concrete ideas about how to support our children in this quest. Dawna shows clearly that we are part of a deficit-oriented society— one that sees what is wrong with our children rather than what is right. She shows that as we begin to shift this thinking to an asset-driven approach, our children and our world can only win.

Decision Making

I HAVE ALWAYS BEEN IN AWE of people who can make quick and bold decisions and never look back. Decisions have never been easy for me. I think that I see too many options and then get hung up with trying to make the perfect decision at the time. One time, long before I became a parent, a friend saw me struggling with making a decision about a move and recommended a book about the subject of decision-making. I went to the bookstore, saw that the book was not there, saw another book by the same author, and before I knew it five minutes had gone by with me trying to decide whether to buy the other book instead! (I went to another bookstore.)

Then I became a parent. I cannot think of another profession that has as many day-to-day decisions to be made. Where is our compass for this navigation? Who do we turn to for help? How do we know whether Nanny 911 or Dr. Phil or a parenting manual has the answers that we are looking for?

As I have actively looked at my beliefs, created space in our life, looked at our motivations, and become a different kind of decision-maker, I have found, with relief, that I really only have one main job as a parent. ***This is simply to see and know my children.*** What greater gift can I give them? It is rare, indeed, that we receive this gift from our own parents. As I come to know this as my job (maybe the only truly vital job) I feel the burden of my fears lifting off my shoulders. I realize that I have a perfectly good compass right within me, and I don't need to rely on the outside clamor to direct me. As we truly see our children, we give ourselves permission to delight in them with all of their passions and all of their gifts, and we in fact do make a difference in the world – certainly not a small thing!

I have found, with relief, that I really only have one main job as a parent. ***This is simply to see and know my children.*** What greater gift can I give them?

Here's What I Know About Myself and My Child:

1. Motivations *(mine)*:

2. Motivations *(child's)*:

3. Temperament *(mine)*:

4. Temperament *(child's)*:

5. Energetic Rhythms *(mine)*:

6. Energetic Rhythms *(child's)*:

7. Gifts *(mine)*:

8. Gifts *(child's)*:

9. Roadblocks:

10. Weakness / Strength:

11. Underlying Assumptions:

12. Vision:

13. Small changes to implement:

The Practice

Creating the Conditions

Scenario 1:

It's 8 PM on a school night and everyone is finally home from their various activities. After a hasty dinner of pizza and salad everyone scatters to attend to things for the next day: homework, discussions of who picks up who when etc. Suddenly, Nancy (the mom) realizes that tomorrow is lesson day for Max, the eight-year-old.

"Max, come down and practice!" she calls up in a pleasant voice she remembers to use.

"Oh man! I'm just starting my math homework!" he calls down.

Nancy ends up taking his violin up to his room, getting it out and saying, "Let's just get this done! I know we're tired. Let's not fuss and just do it." Max grudgingly begins to saw away on his violin and fool around with siren sounds before Nancy completely loses it – shrieking. *(By the way, I didn't have to watch other families to find these scenarios!)*

So, what was wrong with this picture? It's pretty simple to figure out. It's been a long, non-stop day, there is the pressure of preparing for a lesson the next day as well as the added pressure of homework yet undone, and everyone is tired and at the "end of their ropes."

Finding a solution is more difficult. Each family needs to find their way with this. Some solutions that people have discovered will be described shortly.

Some time ago I came across a book about creativity called *Uncommon Genius: Tracing the Creative Impulse With Forty Winners of the MacArthur Award* by Denise Shekerjian (Random House: 1990). The MacArthur Foundation chooses creative people from many fields to receive a large cash award. There is no application for this prize; it is a surprise gift with no strings attached.

One chapter that made a big impression on me is called "Setting up the Conditions." Creative people need certain conditions to be in place to let their ideas come to some kind of form. I have heard friends frequently mutter, "I'm never going to win the lottery. I'm not lucky." Then, when asked if they have ever bought a lottery ticket they admit they never have! This is an extreme example of *not* setting the conditions.

I then began thinking about practicing with my own child. Was it possible for me to set up the conditions for our practice to be successful? I believe this is a missing piece for many families. Like the artists, scientists and entrepreneurs in the book, each of us has our own unique need for certain conditions to be in place so our creativity can flower. I will offer some ideas here, but each parent will find their own.

First, recognize that spending time with music is a much bigger honor than many of us realize. It has been called the "crown jewel" of the arts; music reaches people's hearts in profound ways. This is what we are giving our children. Taking a moment or two to appreciate this before we start the practice creates the conditions for us to be more fully present during the time with our child.

Much of what we explored in the first section of the book sets the conditions as well. Seeing ourselves and our children for who we are allows us to set the conditions as they need to be.

What is the parent's role in setting these conditions? First, of course, we need to be rested and fed, and given the space we need to be out of the swirl of the day-to-day. We can then make some decisions. Sometimes this might make us look like we are the "bad guy" – perhaps insisting on a family rule like only two outside activities per person. Sometimes the decision might be outside the norm: not owning a TV; very limited "screen time;" or homeschooling. Sometimes it comes down to very simple things: choosing a time of day to practice where both of you are fresh, reducing clutter where the practice occurs, or unplugging the phone.

The children are a wonderful reflection of how things are really going. Study of a musical instrument often shines a spotlight on what is a little off-kilter with our relationship or the conditions. Children will tell us through the practice (and many other ways) if everyone is too busy, if people around them are stressed, if there is too little or too much structure, or if the parent is living through the child with unrealized dreams of their own.

BECOME A DETECTIVE

What could happen at home to create optimum conditions for a great practice?

What behaviors do your children tend to show you as a barometer of your relationship? Does one child more than another take on this "job"?

What simple steps could you take to make improvements?

Read on for more ideas about setting conditions.

Practice Organization

Scenario 2:

It's the weekend, and Nancy and Max have found a nice quiet time to practice; the phone is turned off; and both are rested and in good moods. The conditions are right for a terrific practice, and Nancy is determined to get a lot done before the week hits. They plunge in with the new piece and begin drilling the difficult spots. Nancy is proud of herself because she is being very creative: letting Max roll dice to see how many repetitions of difficult spots to do, asking him for his feedback, and alternating between this "spot" practice and playing the whole piece, putting the spot in context. "Really, I am beginning to master my pacing and creativity in these practices," she thinks happily to herself. After about a half an hour of this Max starts getting wiggly, glances at Mom, and then purposely makes mistakes. Nancy doesn't notice this but does feel her anxiety level changing. Suddenly (at least suddenly to Nancy) Max announces that he wants to quit violin. Nancy is dumbfounded.

What went wrong here?

It was going so well! Think of it from the child's point of view. Music is invisible in the first place. There is no clear moment when it is finished – unlike other art forms. Also, Mom or Dad are changeable. One day they might be satisfied with fairly mediocre work (especially if tired or rushed) and on another day they might get in a mood where nothing is ever enough. The child can have trouble gauging the mood of the parent, as well as feel that when the seemingly endless session will stop is out of their control (which is often true). I have come to realize that even a happy practice can quickly come to a bad end because the child feels that the only way to end it is to undermine it.

The three sections (beginning, middle, and end) of the practice have unique aspects to them. I have found helpful information on this organizational aspect of practicing from a book called *The Spirit Of Being Organized* by Pamela Kristan (Red Wheel: 2003). Not only is she a professional organizer, but she is a trained pianist as well. Many of her analogies are musical. I found as I read this book that the ideas offered about organizing the home are applicable to the practice sessions.

THE BEGINNING:

I have always loved the quote, "beginning is half done." Often it feels that this is the most challenging part of any project. Perhaps we remember a difficult ending of the practice the day before or maybe we have missed a few days and dread the way it's going to feel or sound. Sometimes we might feel overwhelmed by the magnitude of what we are trying to accomplish and find it easier to not face it at all. Pamela Kristan suggests that we are wise to make sure that what we do makes a difference.

I have found that the most important thing that I can do for a practice session that will make that difference is to take just a moment and ask myself, "Why am I doing this today?" Every day there is a different answer: sometimes lofty, sometimes mundane. For me, it is often, "So Sarah can express herself through music," or "So Benjamin can find how each little step adds up to something bigger." Sometimes it is, "So I can feel like an organized mother," or "So the kids can get a scholarship for college."

What are some reasons you are offering music to your child?

....

....

....

Keep in mind that the first small step is one moment in time. The next step will then come from the first one. Each step, each moment, will have its own wisdom. You do not have to map out the whole journey ahead of time.

THE MIDDLE:

Start by detaching yourself (*The Spirit of Being Organized,* pg. 20) and simply *observing,* as a "curious anthropologist." Take away any judgment and simply see what works and what doesn't. Take any emotions that come up and simply use them to provide the data in which to shape the practice session. Our "observing self" is always available to us, even during the not-so-easy moments in the practice. Pamela suggests that we:
a) step out of the stream of experience;
b) open our attention;
c) capture whatever information we find, and
d) step back in the stream.

FOR MORE INFORMATION:

The Spirit Of Being Organized by Pamela Kristan (Red Wheel: 2003)

The Inner Game of Tennis by W. Timothy Gallwey (Random House: 1997)

What do you observe in the practice?

Next, remind yourself to let go of expectations while at the same time holding a vision. This will let your joy in the exploration of the moment grow.

What is your vision for your child with music?

What expectation can you drop?

What is your child's vision?

Now acknowledge what you have done (*The Spirit of Being Organized,* pg. 29). See that what you do makes a difference. Find that your forward motion (your movement towards what you want and away from what you don't want) is making a difference. Celebrate the intermediate goals with your child. See what is working before ricocheting your attention onto the next task.

Achieved goals to celebrate along the way:

THE END:

I have found that how the practice ends has a profound impact on the attitude about the next practice (for both parent and child). Pamela Kristan has several ideas for helping the end be successful. First of all, it is important to determine a time frame for the practice session. Many a difficult practice is caused by the child feeling that the session is endless, and not under their control.

Then honor the commitment you have made for what constitutes the end. Do not be tempted to press on for more since it is going well. End on a "high note" where everyone is happy, as Dr. Suzuki recommended.

"Closing down" the practice is a three-step process:
Try this three-step process out with your child. Write down what you discover.

3-STEP PROCESS

1. *Talk about what happened in the practice (especially accomplishments!).*
2. *Look at the next practice. What is the next step?*
3. *Look at the present. What needs to happen to make the transition to "business as usual"?*

1. What just happened? *(past)*

2. What are the next goals? *(future)*

3. What happens to help the transition from practice to the next event? *(present)*

Taking Temperaments Into Consideration In Our Practice

Scenario 3:

Peter (Dad) and Rachel (11) sit down together to practice cello. All looks perfect with this scenario. Both are rested, fed, and happy. Rachel loves the cello and they have a terrific relationship. Peter sits close and leans forward with interest while Rachel plays her Breval Sonata. As she finishes he says, "Great job, why don't you try the first couple of lines watching that your bow stays closer to the bridge?" Rachel bursts into tears.

What is wrong here? On the surface, it is hard to see, but this is the scene I have lived repeatedly – both as a child practicing with my father and as a mother practicing with my daughter. The issue is intensity. When both people are high in intensity, this intensity can literally collide in the air energetically. The child can feel that the parent is actually mad at them when the parent was nothing of the sort!

Here is what I found to be of help with my daughter. (I admit it a little sheepishly, but when I do share this in parent lectures I have parents thank me years later for this advice):

1. Sit across the room.
2. Have something in your hand like a cup of coffee.
3. Turn your body sideways.
4. Even (and I shudder to say this!) flip through a magazine.
5. When you do say something, make it brief and turn away before the child replies.

CAUTION! *These tactics are not for everyone, only for when the parent and child are both intense. My son would be sad if I practiced with him in this way. Each child has their own needs for how the interactions take place.*

Here are other common practice situations that are complicated by temperament traits:

The very persistent child can get totally focused on trying to fix something to the point of feeling locked-in with frustration. Some suggestions for this:

1. Head it off at the pass. Set up clear boundaries with time or repetitions *before* they try it.
2. Let them come up with a way to unlock. They need us to say, "You are a good problem solver. What would your solution to this be?" Find ways to help them let go when caught in a frustrating experience. Sometimes humor might do it, or imagination. Read Mary Sheedy Kurcinka's *Raising Your Spirited Child* (HarperCollins: 1991) and *Raising Your Spirited Child Workbook* (HarperCollins: 1998) for many more helpful hints.

I often run into "slow-to-warm-up" children in what I do because I teach many workshops where I am meeting the children for the first time, and – more importantly – they are meeting me for the first time.

Scenario 4:

I am tuning all the children's violins before a group class, when I see a child clinging to her mother, unwilling to come forward to get her's tuned. They come together, Mom handing me the violin. I chat with them both a little and then say to the child, "You take your time, Mom can be right with you." After the kids all get their spots in their rows I let the child know that there is a special spot for her saved – right near Mom and right next to her friend. I again say, "Take your time," and proceed with class. Invariably she will see the fun she is missing and slip into her spot in a few moments, sometimes after a little more relaxed encouragement from me. What amazes me every time this happens is that often that same child is raising her hand and answering questions after about five more minutes.

Now, if the parent is caught up in the fact that they don't want to waste their money, or they panic that the child will miss the experience, they often try to force the child to participate before they are ready. This always backfires – with the child crying and the parent upset. It takes trust to go with the pace of the child who does not want to dive right in.

Think about some ways that temperament traits show themselves in practice sessions with your child:

Using Motivation, Energetic Rhythms, and Gifts in Our Practice

Scenario 5:

It's time to practice in the Woodruf household and Sally (Mom) is very excited to get to it. It's a beautiful day and she suggests that Katie take her flute outside to the porch to play. Katie doesn't want to and goes to the living room where she always practices. "How about playing some duets first?" asks Sally, reaching for her clarinet. "I just want to get this done," mutters Katie, starting with her scale. Sally suggests using a new tone color – no response. She suggests using a metronome for the etude – rolled eyes. Sally applauds after a piece and gets kicked out of the practice.

What is going on here? Two different energetic rhythms are at work. Katie is in trunk-mode. She wants to simply check off her items and complete her goal of practicing her flute. Sally's energy is from higher in the tree. She is filled with creative options – options that make Kate feel she is being "way-laid" in her attempts to meet her goal. If Sally had been more sensitive to this need she might have been able to suggest one idea or certainly to applaud after a piece, but Katie felt too bombarded to accept *any* option. This also points out something about the gifts and motivations of both people. Sally was motivated to change the routine; Katie was motivated to stick to hers. Sally was using her gifts for creative thinking while Katie was using her abilities to implement a plan. These traits are certainly tied together.

Looking at our gifts can give us many hints about what might motivate us to practice. One child might be motivated by performing. You can line up stuffed animals that each "choose a piece" they want to hear. You can play a surprise for Daddy or Mommy when he or she gets home or make a recording for relatives.

Another child might enjoy the social experience of music making, as my son does. Have friends bring their instruments when they come over. Find a small ensemble for your child to play in. My son loves his string quartet, orchestra, duets with a friend, tour group, summer institutes, and traveling with me to play. These activities with people keep him constantly motivated.

Other children who love keeping busy with their hands and want to understand how things work might love the physics of the instrument, how it's built, or how the vibrations feel to them.

Some children love long term goals, some like extremely short term goals, and some get the best feeling by ticking off each day on their practice chart.

So what happens if the motivations for parent and child are extremely different? What if the parent is a Trunk and the child is a Leaf? First of all, keep in mind that it might be the *parent* that might need the chart to tick off each day! Put it right up on your refrigerator. Then, take a look at how you can "meet in the middle" of the energies in the practice. Let the child help with solutions. For instance, if the child really wants to just play the music in their own little world (slopping through it in your opinion) and you want to get the passage learned for the lesson, come to agreements about how to do both. Perhaps you can alternate these types of activities, or perhaps the child can get some of the playing "their way" done a few minutes before you enter the scene so you don't have to listen to it!

Keep an eye out for other motivators that help you or your child. It really helps me to keep in mind the larger reasons I do this, so taking a few minutes right before the practice to think about why I am doing it today motivates me. If you are a parent who likes praise you could enlist the aid of a partner or another adult who can give you feedback about the consistent job you are doing. Another person might keep a journal and write down all of the successes for that day or periodically make a musical recording to keep track of progress. If the child (or you) loves to bring in creative ideas to the practices, see pages 54 and 59 or check out the sources after these next questions.

MOTIVATION

WHAT MOTIVATES my child?

How can we incorporate this into the practice?

WHAT GIFTS does my child have that we can capitalize on?

MOTIVATION CONTINUED

How can we incorporate this into the practice?

WHAT INFORMATION about the parts of the tree can help our understanding?

How can we incorporate this into the practice?

For More Information:

My Music Journal: A Practicing Companion by Carrie Reuning-Hummel and Jennifer Reuning Myers (Coming soon! See order form in back.)

Helping Parents Practice: Ideas for Making It Easier by Edmund Sprunger (Yes Publishing: 2005) *www.yespublishing.com*

A Soprano On Her Head by Eloise Ristad (Real People Press: 1981)
This is a classic must-read, required for many music students. Eloise Ristad takes a deep look at the perceptions that are unique to each of us. Through this book I learned to never make assumptions about anyone's way of learning or looking at things.

Sensory Tuneups: A guided journal of sensory experiences for performers of all ages by Kay Hooper (AllSense Press: 2005) *www.allsense.com*
A practice and performing workbook that guides you to learn more about your music-making process through seeing, hearing, moving, and thinking. Appropriate for children of any age with guidance, or ten years and up on their own.

Practicing Principles

Ingredients for Excellence:
Listening, Reviewing, Attention to Tone

LISTENING:

This is a magic ingredient for good progress. If the sounds of the piece that you are working on are already "in your ear", then a missed note or rhythm will likely loom out as an error, never to be repeated again. The days are gone when we as teachers and parents need to circle the notes and mark the music week in and week out. Dr. Suzuki told the story of an experiment he tried with two young boys who were playing the same piece, both quite poorly. Student #1 was sent home with instructions: all week practice nothing but the piece. Student #2 was told to *only listen* to the piece – not to even play it once.

I ask my students to answer the question of who came in playing it better. Many answer student #1, thinking that it *must* be the one who practiced more. Of course the answer is student #2 – the one who then heard what the right notes were. The first boy just learned his mistakes even better.

How can we add more listening to our days?

....

....

....

....

....

....

Goal:

....

....

....

....

REVIEWING:

If we are always turning the page just as we get the notes learned to a piece we will

- never have a real comfort level with that piece, or *any* piece for that matter, and
- never have anything ready to perform.

We are able to experiment musically when we know the notes to the extent that we are not "supervising" them any more. When we know the notes, each time we play the piece we are able to be creative in a new way. Concert artists provide a good example of this. They have many concertos kept at a level where if another artist cancels, they are ready to substitute at any moment.

There are many ways to have reviewing be fun and not mindless. A favorite of mine is the jar idea: write down pieces onto slips of paper that you fold and put in a jar. In another jar, place ways of playing the pieces. Mix silly and serious ideas like, "Play with your eyes closed, play too slow or too fast, imagine your tone is a color, concentrate on your left hand." etc. etc.

Some reviewing ideas to try:

Goals for fitting these 3 things into our practice:

ATTENTION TO TONE:

The more we are accustomed to the active listening that hearing (or feeling) the resonance of our tone requires, the more we are apt to hear correct pitches and rhythms as well as intonation (playing in tune). I have found that beginning the lessons and practices with opening our ears to this makes all the difference for the remainder of the lesson. Suzuki said "Tone is the living soul." He felt that listening this deeply also had ramifications for listening to each other as human beings.

I often find that a good way to focus on tone is to talk about what "color" the tone is. If the child is banging on the piano, there is no way they can produce a pale pink tone. If the violinist's bow is slipping over the fingerboard there is no way the sound can be deep, purple velvet. This is a very different approach from working on technique (as in "get your bow closer to the bridge") but it is more fun, and allows the child to be the active listener instead of you!

Remember that these three keys to excellence (listening, reviewing, and tone) need to be priorities. They are often the first to be eliminated when life gets busy. I tell my families that if they have just five minutes to practice on a particular day, they should fit these three things in instead of panicking to learn the new piece.

CONSISTENCY:

Try to practice at the same time each day, if possible. While not necessary in all families, consistency often helps create an easy-going and unquestioned routine. Some times that can work well are in the morning before school (many families favor this); immediately after school and a quick snack; before other activities; or between dinner and dessert. Some families have great success splitting up the practice. For instance, they might review in the morning, listen to a CD in the car, and work on newer material right after school.

Keep in mind that every day that you skip a practice makes the next day more difficult. This is partly because we get out of the routine and partly because we fear we won't sound or feel as good when we come back to it.

Be careful not to use practice as a punishment. This can be subtle, as in "Since it's your birthday you don't have to practice," or "When you turn sixteen you don't have to practice." We have a family policy to practice everyday– even if it's only for five minutes.

Try having a meeting with your child and decide together about what times might work best for your practices. Of course, have your child choose from structures that you offer as possibilities. Keep in mind that this may need to be revisited from time to time.

What did we find to try?

MOOD PREPARATION:

Preparing the mood is important for both you and your child before both practice and lessons. First, take a couple of minutes to remind yourself why you are making this effort for your child. Look at your child as an important person, separate from yourself, whose self-esteem will be strengthened by the small steps of music study. Then take a few quiet moments with your child to discuss some of the important points of the lesson. Perhaps listen to a tape of the lesson, or to a recording of the piece being studied. On the way to the lesson you can do the same things or listen to any music and discuss how it makes you feel, what color it reminds you of, etc.

Keep track of a week's practice with attention to mood preparation and note any changes here:

MODEL THE PRACTICE AFTER THE LESSON:

I usually try to alternate activities in my teaching, for instance standing vs. sitting, fast pace vs. slow pace, or "performing" (with no interruptions) vs. working on one small passage. A delicate part of the art of teaching is working on one point at a time so that we are not bombarding the student with too much to think about. This sometimes means ignoring mistakes and areas that could be improved, which can be extremely challenging. But if I can do it, you can do it! Keep the atmosphere positive with room for experimenting, questioning, analyzing, and mistakes. Try to stop before it is the child's idea. Try to anticipate moods (yours and your child's) and counteract challenging moods with a game or a shortened practice.

Watch your child's teacher with new eyes over the next few weeks. What techniques used in the lesson could you incorporate into your practice?

What do you see that would *not* work at home? Keep in mind that *all* of us would do well to talk less:

ASK, DON'T TELL:

Ask, "What did you hear that time?" Better yet, ask what they would like to think about when they play the piece. Determining goals beforehand saves a lot of time and helps you, as the practice partner, resist the urge to correct in the midst of the piece. Any question that asks them to be the active listener, the person in the "driver's seat," is the way to go. One idea that has worked for me is, "Stop if you hear a tone you don't like (such as scratchy, 'soapy,' or 'thuddy') and we'll see who hears it first." Usually the child doesn't even have to stop this time because they have taken on the responsibility of listening, and they don't allow the unwelcome sound to occur.

Other questions to try are, "Do you want to do this activity 5 or 10 times?" (give a framework) or "How many times do you think you need to do that passage so you never goof it again?" You may be wondering, "What if my child answers 'Once' to that question?" What I do, as a teacher, is just go with that answer. I will say something like, "Let's try it and see if you are the kind of learner where once will be enough." Then when I see them again I do not mention their prediction, I just have them play the piece with the passage in question. Inevitably they do make the mistake again and I can say, "Okay, we found from this experiment that once wasn't enough. How many repetitions would you like to try next?" The idea is to offer choices and responsibility along with respect for their thoughts and ideas.

List "ask, don't tell" ideas that you and your child come up with for future practices:

Use this space to write down what happens when you try out "ask, don't tell" ideas:

CREATIVITY:

These ideas may work well for some children but not all. Keep your ideas fun and not manipulative. Let your child choose which works for them. Many of the ideas help the invisible (music) become more concrete. Above all, HAVE FUN!!!!

1. **Charts.** Have the child draw something to document each accomplishment.
2. **Perform.** Play for anyone and everyone! "Let's practice this new spot and then show it to Daddy tonight." Gather together stuffed animals and let them each "choose" a piece or activity. Invite a friend who plays an instrument over to play music. Make an audio recording or a video for the grandparents or other far-away relatives.
3. **Review.** Write down pieces and activities on slips of paper and pull them out of a hat or jar. Mix silly ideas with serious ones.
4. Before the practice, write down a **"To-Do List"** for that day. Let the child cross each item off. (This helps to keep practice from feeling endless to a child.)
5. Work on making your language **respectful.** Tape yourself practicing with your child and analyze it.
6. **Celebrate** small achievements. (This is different from a reward, which is used to motivate achievement in advance, because it happens afterwards as a response.) Go out to dinner to celebrate when a difficult piece has been learned. Go to a concert as a family (especially if you find out in advance what will be performed and can listen to the pieces first). If your child loves to perform, have a mini-recital at home with some friends and family and serve a treat afterwards.

Fostering Ownership of the Instrument From Day One

Scenario 6:

Time to practice in the Adams household. Heidi (Mom) calls Maggie (8) in and by the time Maggie rounds the corner, Mom has her violin out and is rosining the bow. Maggie proceeds to sag into a chair and begins to whine about practicing. Heidi tells her that she can have a piece of candy if she practices with "a good attitude." This cheers Maggie up and she begins her practice. As her piece begins Heidi reminds her about her bow hold. "Get your pinkie bent!" she says several times as the piece progresses. "Don't rush!" "Bow hold!" "Low 2!" "Bend your pinkie!" etc. etc. "Watch your bow – don't let it over the fingerboard." (Towards the end of the piece) "Maggie, why are you looking at me? Stop it! Look at your bow!"

This is based on a real-life practice that I observed at a summer Suzuki institute. What was so striking was that after absolutely barraging her daughter with commands, the mom was upset that her daughter was looking at her!

The preceding scenario shows quite the opposite of the sense of ownership we all hope that our children have with their music.

When I was young I had all kinds of "tricks" for trying to avoid practicing. One time I decided to tape-record my practice session for use on other days (I was practicing alone by then). I taped a very careful practice session, taking care to practice slowly, work with the metronome, repeat spots numerous times – all the things I did not normally do. Then the next day I went up to my room, found a favorite book, and pressed the play button on the tape player. About five minutes later I heard from downstairs, "Turn off the tape recorder and get practicing!" Foiled again.

In retrospect I can see that I spent many years as a violinist who did not "own" what I was doing. Often I was waiting for someone else to tell me what to do or to tell me how to improve something. I didn't really start taking ownership until I was about fifteen – ten years after beginning lessons. I think that is much too long.

I tried a very different route with my children and it has really paid off. I will share some ideas here.

It's subtle, but from the very first day of their lessons you can be sending the message to them that this is *theirs*. Have your children carry their own instrument (unless it's a piano or a cello in a flimsy case), get it out themselves, and get it prepared. Let them help with decision making as much as possible: when in the day to practice, how to organize the practice, and how to use motivators.

Most of us are not purely self-motivated. It is a rare student who cannot wait to practice every day. Recognize this and don't think that something is wrong when your child just doesn't feel like practicing. Try to set up an environment where practicing every day is simply what happens. Our attitude was that even if it was sometimes just for five minutes that day, this was fine.

Being prepared for the lesson is important if the student is to feel great about themselves and the instrument. When we go in feeling under-prepared and try to hide it from the teacher, it is hard to feel good about owning our role in it. Share the fact that it has been a rough week with the teacher so they will know, but also let the teacher become the person that the child "answers to" when good practicing is not happening at home. Sometimes taking a step back from being the "enforcer" as a parent can make a huge difference in the child's ownership.

Respectfully and honestly cheer your children on. Let them own their learning, but set the conditions so that they will be successful.

There is a balance to find between being over-involved and apathetic as a practicing parent. An example of this is what I see each year when I visit thirty-five second grade classrooms, both as a docent and as a quartet musician in a music education outreach program. It is amazing to see the difference in enthusiasm in the kids depending on how much ownership the teachers allow them. The teachers who sit right with the children – giving their rapt attention to the music, allowing the children to actively participate – have classrooms that foster enthusiasm for learning. In contrast, occasionally a teacher begins to take over the whole experience, leaving no room for the children to participate. There are also the handful of teachers who sit at their desks catching up with work or have a substitute teacher come in. The children in these classrooms show the same lack of enthusiasm as their teachers do.

Respectfully and honestly cheer your children on. Let them own their learning, but set the conditions so that they will be successful. Show them *your* own passion for learning. Show them yourself grappling with something new. This will be the best model for ownership – to see you doing this because you *care*, not because you feel guilty or dutiful.

Taking a Step Back as Our Child Progresses

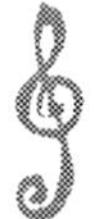  

FROM DAY ONE as we foster our child's responsibility and ownership of music, the ultimate goal is that music will be *theirs* some day.

It can be tricky to know when and how to begin stepping out of the practice sessions, as a parent. One thing that is clear is that if you have been careful to let the child explore and direct much of their learning from the beginning, it can be a lot easier to take a step back.

The first steps may happen very gradually – for instance, being in the next room while the child is doing their review. I would often be in the kitchen and call in, "Wow, your tone was so strong I could hear it over the running water!"

The teacher can help out a lot all along the way. I have found it very beneficial to give a specific assignment to the parent, such as being in charge of watching the finger position for particular pieces. Besides allowing the parent to begin to take a "backseat" to the child's ownership of the practice, this is also helpful when the child really doesn't want to hear from the parent at all.

When does this stepping back happen? It completely varies, depending on the relationship between parent and child, as well as the goals of the teacher. Some teachers have a certain age in mind when the parent stops attending the lesson, others do not. I look for the time when it seems important that the student and I establish our own relationship, although sometimes this doesn't seem to *ever* be an issue. It can be great to have the parent there as an appreciative audience and note-taker.

Some years back I was teaching a twelve-year-old girl who was treating me fairly rudely. I decided not to take this behavior personally because I believed it was a reflection of what was going on between her and her mom, rather than of our teacher-student relationship. I got up my nerve and asked the mom (also a music teacher) to stop coming to the lessons for a while. She was very sad to have this practice relationship change, but agreed to it. Overnight the relationship between me and my student changed. We laughed about boys, talked about school, and even got some work done with the violin. After a few months we invited her mom back. She was so glad to get to sit and simply enjoy her daughter! She later told me that the experience taught her a lot about letting go at a crucial time, and she feels that the teenage years went more smoothly because of that lesson.

I can't emphasize enough what a valuable role the teacher can play during this time when the student is becoming more independent. Inevitably practice gets sloppier and more careless for awhile. It can really help if the teacher becomes the person that the student answers to. If the practice is obviously not what it needs to be, the teacher can set forth some ground rules about what needs to be happening at home. I have also had success with making practice tapes – usually only needed for a few weeks. During the lesson I set up a tape recorder (or video) for my students to use at home, and I direct the practice. "Start measure......, play it with me: ready, go. Turn off the tape recorder and play it 15 more times." etc. It takes quite a bit of organization within the lesson but is often worth it.

One very successful period of time in my practice with my Dad was during the course of a year or so when I was thirteen or fourteen. He would meet with me at the beginning of the practice and help me to plan my practice time and determine my goals. Then he would leave for about 45 minutes. When he returned, I would show him what I had accomplished while he was gone. I liked this a lot because I had something concrete to demonstrate what I had learned. Given the invisibility of music, this can often be an issue for people- there is always more to do, and often nothing *tangible* to show that your work is complete.

Another idea is to ask the child what they would like your role to be. My daughter really liked me to simply be in the room with her as a companion, not as a practice partner. My sister's daughter was changeable. Sometimes she wanted help with a specific issue, or help organizing her practice session. Other times she simply wanted a companion, as my daughter preferred. Learning the importance of asking what was desired helped my sister stop wasting time (and good moods) with guess-work.

IDEAS:

When You Know the Practice is Going to Be Rough

SOMEHOW, I USUALLY KNOW IN ADVANCE of the practice when things are not going to go well. Something in the air, I guess. What I have found is that those are the times to "head it off at the pass." I do this also in my teaching when the child comes in upset about something and I know that it will take most of the half hour lesson for them to feel that they can focus.

One strategy that I use is to blame the tension on myself. "I'm sorry, I hardly have any time today. We're only going to have time for three things." Then we write down the three things with the child choosing the first item, me choosing the 2nd (what *I* really want to accomplish), and the child choosing the final item. I then let the child cross off each item as we accomplish it. This has saved many a practice and lesson for me!

I'm also following this strategy when I say, "I have been having a really bad day. Would you play me a beautiful piece to cheer me up?" Then I simply listen (with no correcting) and the child feels wonderful that they have cheered me up.

Other techniques that can really help are to allow no criticism to enter into the practice at all or to use the jar idea of picking slips of paper for pieces and activities to do side-by-side. These ideas turn off the "heat" within the practice.

My favorite way to "head the bad moods off at the pass" is to change routines. Here are some ideas I have used:

- Play in the bathroom (nice acoustics!).
- Take a bath (for relaxation) and then play.
- Parent "faints" when something sounds great.
- Parent tries to "trick" student with a challenge (that they know the student can do).
- Practice in a different order.
- Do all one thing: just tone, just review, or just give a concert.

You might say to all these ideas, "But I'm not that creative," or "I'm too tired to be creative when it's time to practice." That's what this book is all about! Do the figuring out when you are in better shape to do so, then leave this book near by for one of those desperate moments. Keep in mind that you can also enlist the aid of your child for creativity. If you are truly in this together, if the child feels a sense of ownership in the practice and feels respected and "seen" by you, you will be amazed by how you can both turn things around as a team.

I wish you joy on your journey together!

Are the proper conditions set for the practice?

Do I have a good understanding of my organizing principles?

Beginning/Middle/End notes to remember:

Notes on our temperaments and how we can work together:

Notes on our motivation in the practice:

Notes on our energetic rhythms: How can we meet in the middle?

Notes on using our gifts in the practice:

Ideas about Practicing Principles (Ingredients for Excellence: listening; review; tone; consistency; mood preparation; modeling the practice after the lesson; ask don't tell; and creativity):

Ideas for Fostering Musical Ownership:

Ideas about Stepping Back:

"Heading it off at the pass" ideas:

Books to read:

Ideas from my child:

Main things I am already doing well in our practice:

Ideas about which direction to go with improvement:

Creative ideas to try when things are rough:

Practice Planner

Date ....

Conditions set?

....

....

....

Why am I doing this today?

....

....

....

Observations:

....

....

....

Acknowledgments:

....

....

....

Future Planning:

....

....

....

Practice Planner

Date ....

Conditions set?

....

....

....

Why am I doing this today?

....

....

....

Observations:

....

....

....

Acknowledgments:

....

....

....

Future Planning:

....

....

....

Practice Planner

Date ....

Conditions set?

....

....

....

Why am I doing this today?

....

....

....

Observations:

....

....

....

Acknowledgments:

....

....

....

Future Planning:

....

....

....

Practice Planner

Date ....

Conditions set?

....

....

....

Why am I doing this today?

....

....

....

Observations:

....

....

....

Acknowledgments:

....

....

....

Future Planning:

....

....

....

Bibliography

Armstrong, Thomas. 7 Kinds of Smart: Identifying and Developing Your Many Intelligences. New York: Plume, 1993

Fried, Robert L. The Passionate Learner. Boston, MA: Beacon Press, 2002

Gallwey, W. Timothy. The Inner Game of Tennis. New York: Random House, 1997

Gardner, Howard. Multiple Intelligences: The Theory in Practice. New York: Basic Books, 1993

Holt, John. How Children Fail. New York: Dell Publishing Co. Inc, 1964

Holt, John. Learning All The Time. Reading, MA: Addison-Wesley Publishing Co. Inc., 1989

Holt, John. What Do I Do Monday? New York: E.P. Dutton & Co. Inc., 1970

Hooper, Kay. Sensory Tuneups: A Guided Journal of Sensory Experiences for Performers of All Ages. Selinsgrove, PA: AllSense Press, 2005

Jacobsen, Mary-Elaine. Liberating Everyday Genius. New York: Ballantine, 1999

Johnson, Anne and Goodman, Vic. The Essence of Parenting. New York: Crossroads Publishing Co., 1998

Kohn, Alfie. Punished By Rewards. Boston, MA: Houghton Mifflin Co., 1993

Kohn, Alfie. Unconditional Parenting. New York: Atria Books, 2005

Kristan, Pamela. The Spirit of Being Organized. Boston, MA: Red Wheel, 2003

Kurcinka, Mary Sheedy. Kids, Parents and Power Struggles. New York: Harper Paperbacks, 2001

Kurcinka, Mary Sheedy. Raising Your Spirited Child. New York: HarperCollins Publishers, 1991

Kurcinka, Mary Sheedy. Raising Your Spirited Child Workbook. New York: HarperCollins Publishers, 1998

Laney, Marti Olsen. The Hidden Gifts of the Introverted Child. New York: Workman Publishing Co., 2005

Levine, Mel. A Mind At A Time. New York: Simon & Schuster, 2002

Markova, Dawna. How Your Child *Is* Smart. Berkely, CA: Conari Press, 1992

Markova, Dawna. The Smart Parenting Revolution. New York: Ballantine Books: 2005

Reuning-Hummel, Carrie and Myers, Jennifer Reuning. My Music Journal: A Practicing Companion. Ithaca, NY: Sound Carries Press, 2006

Ristad, Eloise. A Soprano On Her Head. Moab, UT: Real People Press, 1982

Shekerjian, Denise. Uncommon Genius: Tracing the Creative Impulse With Forty Winners of the MacArthur Award. New York: Random House, 1990

Sher, Barbara. Live the Life You Love. New York: Dell Publishing, 1996

Sher, Barbara. Refuse to Choose. London: Rodale, 2006

Sprunger, Edmund. Helping Parents Practice: Ideas for Making It Easier. St. Louis, MO: Yes Publishing, 2005

Suzuki, Shinichi. Ability Development From Age Zero. Translation by Mary Louise Nagata. Athens, OH: Senzay Edition/Ability Development Associates, Inc., Subsidiary of Accura Music, 1981

Suzuki, Shinichi. Nurtured By Love: The Classic Approach to Talent Education. Translation by Waltraud Suzuki. Secaucus, NJ: Summy Birchard, Inc., 1983

Willis, Mariaemma and Victoria Kindle Hodson. Discover Your Child's Learning Style. California: Prima Lifestyles, 1999

About the Author

Carrie Reuning-Hummel began the study of the violin at the age of five with her parents, Joan and Sanford Reuning in Ithaca, N.Y. She was one of the first Suzuki students in the U.S., studied with Shinichi Suzuki on numerous occasions, and has been a member of the Suzuki teaching family for over thirty years. She has taught at hundreds of institutes and workshops throughout the continental U.S. as well as in Hawaii, Puerto Rico, Canada, Mexico, Bermuda, and Israel. In 1986, she was honored to receive the Shar Distinguished Young Teacher Award. Carrie received a BA.in Psychology at the University of Iowa in 1989.

As an internationally known teacher and a certified Suzuki teacher trainer, Carrie advises both parents and teachers how to make the most of the unique parent/child partnership that is integral to the Suzuki method. With humor and heart, Carrie uses simple techniques that turn music lessons into a powerful vehicle for raising purposeful, self-confident, and musical kids. Parents leave Carrie's parent education sessions with a new appreciation of their own gifts, a deeper understanding of their children's gifts and temperaments, and an action plan for happier practice sessions in the future.

Carrie currently serves on the national Board of Directors of the Suzuki Association of the Americas, is a professional violist, and keeps quite busy homeschooling her two children.

Carrie is delighted to offer parent workshops, lectures and private consultations both in person and by phone. For more information and to see her upcoming schedule, see www.soundcarries.com or e-mail her at carrierhum@twcny.rr.com

CPSIA information can be obtained at www.ICGtesting.com
Printed in the USA
BVOW051129030613

322293BV00002B/42/A